Common CORE WritingtoTexts

W9-ASZ-135

Table of Contents

Introduction

What Is the Common Core?

The Common Core State Standards are an initiative by states to set shared, consistent, and clear criteria for what students are expected to learn. This helps teachers and parents know what they need to do to help students. The standards are designed to be rigorous and pertinent to the real world. They reflect the knowledge and skills that young people need for success in college and careers.

If your state has joined the Common Core State Standards Initiative, then teachers are required to incorporate these standards into their lesson plans. Students need targeted practice in order to meet grade-level standards and expectations, and thereby be promoted to the next grade.

What Does It Mean to Write to Texts?

One of the most important instructional shifts in the Common Core State Standards is writing to texts, or sources. What exactly does this mean? Haven't standardized assessments always used reading texts as a springboard to writing? Yes, but the required writing hasn't always been DEPENDENT on the key ideas and details in a text.

A prompt that is non-text-dependent asks students to rely on prior knowledge or experience. In fact, students could likely carry out the writing without reading the text at all. The writing does not need to include ideas, information, and key vocabulary from the text.

Writing to texts requires students to analyze, clarify, and cite information they read in the text. The writing reveals whether students have performed a close reading, because it is designed to elicit ideas, information, and key vocabulary from the text as well as students' own evidence-based inferences and conclusions. These are all skills that prepare them for the grades ahead, college, the workplace, and real-world applications in their adult daily lives.

An example of a passage with non-text-dependent and text-dependent sample prompts is provided on page 3.

Simple Machines

1. A simple machine is a tool that does work with one movement. It has few or no moving parts.

2. You use simple machines all the time, too. If you have opened a door, eaten with a spoon, cut with scissors, or zipped up a zipper, you have used a simple machine.

3. Life would be very different if we did not have machines. Work would be much harder, and playing wouldn't be as fun.

Standard	Sample Prompt: Non-Text-Dependent	Sample Prompt: Text-Dependent
W.1.1 (Opinion/ Argument)	Do you prefer zippers, buttons, buckles, or another type of fastener for your clothing? Why?	The author makes three claims in the last paragraph. Choose one and tell whether you agree or disagree. Support your opinion with facts from the text.
W.1.2 (Informative/ Explanatory)	Think about a machine you have used to do a task. How did you use it? How did using the machine make the task easier?	Explain what a simple machine is. Use details from the text to support your explanation.
W.1.3 (Narrative)	Write a story in which a character invents a machine that no one has seen or heard of before.	Imagine that all the machines mentioned in the passage disappeared one day. Write a story about how your life was different that day.

Using This Book

How Does This Book Help Students?

This book is organized into three main sections: Writing Mini-Lessons, Practice Texts with Prompts, and Rubrics and Assessments. All mini-lessons and practice pages are self-contained and may be used in any order that meets the needs of students. The elements of this book work together to provide students with the tools they need to be able to master the range of skills and application as required by the Common Core.

1. Mini-Lessons for Opinion/Argument, Informative/Explanatory, and Narrative Writing

Writing mini-lessons prepare students to use writing as a way to state and support opinions, demonstrate understanding of the subjects they are studying, and convey real and imagined experiences. The mini-lessons are organized in the order of the standards, but you may wish to do them with your class in an order that matches your curriculum. For each type of writing the first mini-lesson covers responding to literature, while the second mini-lesson models how to respond to informational text.

Each mini-lesson begins with a lesson plan that provides step-by-step instruction.

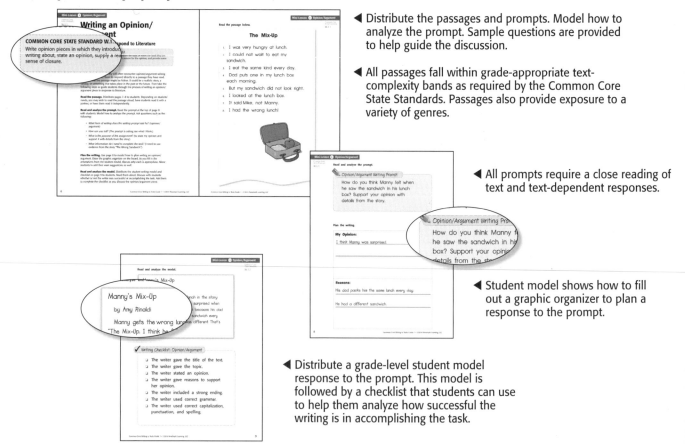

◀ Distribute the passages and prompts. Model how to analyze the prompt. Sample questions are provided to help guide the discussion.

◀ All passages fall within grade-appropriate text-complexity bands as required by the Common Core State Standards. Passages also provide exposure to a variety of genres.

◀ All prompts require a close reading of text and text-dependent responses.

◀ Student model shows how to fill out a graphic organizer to plan a response to the prompt.

◀ Distribute a grade-level student model response to the prompt. This model is followed by a checklist that students can use to help them analyze how successful the writing is in accomplishing the task.

2. Practice Texts with Prompts

Passages and prompts provide students with real experience writing to a text. Each passage is followed by three text-dependent prompts: Opinion/Argument, Informative/Explanatory, and Narrative. On each prompt page, students are also provided with a graphic organizer to help them plan their writing.

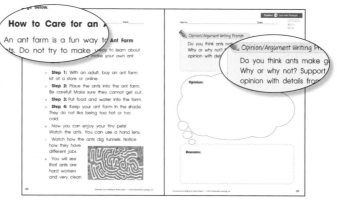

You may wish to assign a particular prompt, have students choose one, or have them execute each type of writing over a longer period of time. For each type of writing, you can distribute a corresponding checklist to help students plan and evaluate their writing.

For more information on how to use this section, see page 30. Also see page 115 for how to use the prompts with students in all developmental stages of writing.

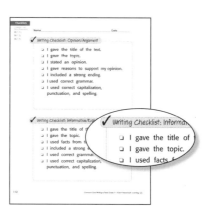

3. Rubrics and Assessments

The section includes Evaluation Rubrics to guide your assessment and scoring of students' responses. Based on your observations of students' writing, use the differentiated rubrics. These are designed to help you conduct meaningful conferences with students and will help differentiate your interactions to match students' needs.

For each score a student receives in the Evaluation Rubrics, responsive prompts are provided. These gradual-release prompts scaffold writers toward mastery of each writing type.

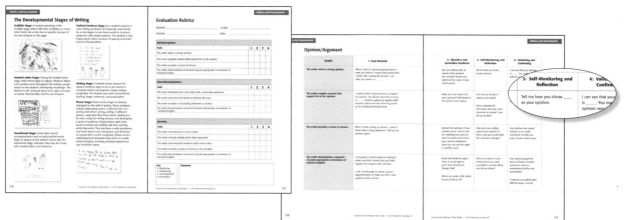

COMMON CORE
STATE STANDARD
W.1.1

Writing an Opinion/ Argument

Mini-Lesson 1: **Respond to Literature**

> **COMMON CORE STATE STANDARD W.1.1**
> Write opinion pieces in which they introduce the topic or name the book they are writing about, state an opinion, supply a reason for the opinion, and provide some sense of closure.

Explain to students that an opinion is what someone thinks or believes. It should be supported by facts and details. Tell them that they can write opinion pieces about something they have read. They might have to give an opinion about a realistic story, a fantasy, or something that takes place in the past or the future. Then take the following steps to guide students through the process of writing an opinion/argument piece in response to literature.

Read the passage. Distribute pages 7–8 to students. Depending on students' needs, you may wish to read the passage aloud, have students read it with a partner, or have them read it independently.

Read and analyze the prompt. Read the prompt at the top of page 8 with students. Model how to analyze the prompt. Ask questions such as the following:

- *What form of writing does the writing prompt ask for?* (opinion/ argument)
- *How can you tell?* (The prompt is asking me what I think.)
- *What is the purpose of the assignment?* (to state my opinion and support it with details from the story)
- *What information do I need?* (I need to use details from the story "The Mix-Up.")

Plan the writing. Use page 8 to model how to plan writing an opinion/ argument. Draw the graphic organizer on the board. As you fill in the annotations from the student model, discuss why each is appropriate. Allow students to add their own suggestions as well.

Read and analyze the model. Distribute the student writing model and checklist on page 9 to students. Read them aloud. Discuss with students whether or not the writer was successful at accomplishing the task. Ask them to complete the checklist as you discuss the opinion/argument piece.

COMMON CORE
STATE STANDARD

W.1.1

Read the passage below.

The Mix-Up

1. I was very hungry at lunch.

2. I could not wait to eat my sandwich.

3. I eat the same kind every day.

4. Dad puts one in my lunch box each morning.

5. But my sandwich did not look right.

6. I looked at the lunch box.

7. It said Mike, not Manny.

8. I had the wrong lunch!

COMMON CORE
STATE STANDARD
W.1.1

Read and analyze the prompt.

Opinion/Argument Writing Prompt

How do you think Manny felt when he saw the sandwich in his lunch box? Support your opinion with details from the story.

Plan the writing.

My Opinion:
I think Manny was surprised.
Reasons:
His dad packs him the same lunch every day.
He had a different sandwich.

Read and analyze the model.

Manny's Mix-Up

by Amy Rinaldi

Manny gets the wrong lunch in "The Mix-Up." I think he feels surprised. This is because his dad packs him the same kind of sandwich every day. But on this day it was different. That's why he is surprised.

✔ Writing Checklist: Opinion/Argument

- ❏ The writer gave the title of the text.
- ❏ The writer gave the topic.
- ❏ The writer stated an opinion.
- ❏ The writer gave reasons to support her opinion.
- ❏ The writer included a strong ending.
- ❏ The writer used correct grammar.
- ❏ The writer used correct capitalization, punctuation, and spelling.

COMMON CORE
STATE STANDARD
W.1.1

Writing an Opinion/ Argument

Mini-Lesson 2: Respond to Informational Text

COMMON CORE STATE STANDARD W.1.1
Write opinion pieces in which they introduce the topic or name the book they are writing about, state an opinion, supply a reason for the opinion, and provide some sense of closure.

Explain to students that an opinion is what someone thinks or believes. It should be supported by facts and details. Tell them that they can write opinion pieces about something they have read. They might have to give an opinion about science or social studies, a how-to passage, a biography or an autobiography, or a digital source. Then take the following steps to guide students through the process of writing an opinion/argument piece in response to an informational text.

Read the passage. Distribute pages 11–12 to students. Depending on students' needs, you may wish to read the passage aloud, have students read it with a partner, or have them read it independently.

Read and analyze the prompt. Read the prompt at the top of page 12 with students. Model how to analyze the prompt. Ask questions such as the following:

- *What form of writing does the writing prompt ask for?* (opinion/ argument)

- *How can you tell?* (The prompt is asking me whether I think people liked Johnny Appleseed.)

- *What is the purpose of the assignment?* (to state my opinion and support it with details from the text)

- *What information do I need?* (I need to use details from the story "Johnny Appleseed.")

Plan the writing. Use page 12 to model how to plan writing an opinion/ argument. Draw the graphic organizer on the board. As you fill in the annotations from the student model, discuss why each is appropriate. Allow students to add their own suggestions as well.

Read and analyze the model. Distribute the student writing model and checklist on page 13 to students. Read them aloud. Discuss with students whether or not the writer was successful at accomplishing the task. Ask them to complete the checklist as you discuss the opinion/argument piece.

Read the passage below.

Johnny Appleseed

1. Johnny Appleseed lived many years ago.

2. His real name was John Chapman.

3. He worked for an apple farmer.

4. The farmer taught him how to grow apple trees.

5. Johnny liked to help people.

6. Johnny traveled from place to place.

7. He taught people how to grow apple trees.

8. Johnny became famous.

9. People thought he was nice.

10. They wanted to meet him.

COMMON CORE
STATE STANDARD
W.1.1

Read and analyze the prompt.

> Opinion/Argument Writing Prompt
>
> Do you think people liked Johnny Appleseed? Why or why not? Support your opinion with details from the text.

Plan the writing.

Do you think people liked Johnny Appleseed?
Yes.
Why or why not?
He taught them how to grow apple trees.
He was nice.
They wanted to meet him.

Why People Liked Johnny Appleseed

by Miguel Sanchez

I read "Johnny Appleseed." I think people liked Johnny Appleseed a lot. Johnny taught them to grow apple trees. People thought he was nice. They wanted to meet him. These are the reasons why I think people liked him.

✔ Writing Checklist: Opinion/Argument

- ❑ The writer gave the title of the text.
- ❑ The writer gave the topic.
- ❑ The writer stated an opinion.
- ❑ The writer gave reasons to support his opinion.
- ❑ The writer included a strong ending.
- ❑ The writer used correct grammar.
- ❑ The writer used correct capitalization, punctuation, and spelling.

COMMON CORE
STATE STANDARD
W.1.2

Writing an Informative/ Explanatory Text

Mini-Lesson 3: **Respond to Literature**

> **COMMON CORE STATE STANDARD W.1.2**
> Write informative/explanatory texts in which they name a topic, supply some facts about the topic, and provide some sense of closure.

Explain to students that they can write for the purpose of informing or explaining. Tell them that they can write informative/explanatory texts about something they have read. They might have to write information or explain something about a realistic story, a fantasy, or something that takes place in the past or the future. Then take the following steps to guide students through the process of informative/explanatory writing in response to literature.

Read the passage. Distribute pages 15–16 to students. Depending on students' needs, you may wish to read the passage aloud, have students read it with a partner, or have them read it independently.

Read and analyze the prompt. Read the prompt at the top of page 16 with students. Model how to analyze the prompt. Ask questions such as the following:

- *What form of writing does the writing prompt ask for?* (informative)

- *How can you tell?* (The prompt is asking me why Crow puts rocks in the pitcher of water.)

- *What is the purpose of the assignment?* (to give an explanation and support it with details from the story)

- *What information do I need?* (I need to use details from the story "The Crow and the Pitcher.")

Plan the writing. Use page 16 to model how to plan writing an informative/ explanatory piece. Draw the graphic organizer on the board. As you fill in the annotations from the student model, discuss why each is appropriate. Allow students to add their own suggestions as well.

Read and analyze the model. Distribute the student writing model and checklist on page 17 to students. Read it aloud. Discuss with students whether or not the writer was successful at accomplishing the task. Ask them to complete the checklist as you discuss the informative/explanatory piece.

Read the passage below.

The Crow and the Pitcher

1.   Crow was thirsty. He saw a pitcher. But only a little bit of water was left.

2.   Crow put his beak into the pitcher. He could not reach the water.

3.   Then Crow had an idea. He put some rocks in the pitcher. This made the water get higher. He put more rocks in the pitcher.

4.   Now the water was very high. Crow drank the water.

COMMON CORE
STATE STANDARD
W.1.2

Read and analyze the prompt.

Informative/Explanatory Writing Prompt

Why does Crow put rocks in the pitcher? Use details from the story to support your answer.

Plan the writing.

Crow puts rocks in the pitcher.

Reasons:

The water is too low.

Crow can't reach it with his beak.

The rocks make the water get higher.

 Common Core Writing to Texts Grade 1 • ©2014 Newmark Learning, LLC

Read and analyze the model.

Why the Crow Puts Rocks in the Pitcher

by Hannah Smith

The crow in "The Crow and the Pitcher" is thirsty. But the water in the pitcher is too low. Crow puts rocks in the water. This makes the water higher. Then Crow can drink it. That's why Crow puts rocks in the pitcher.

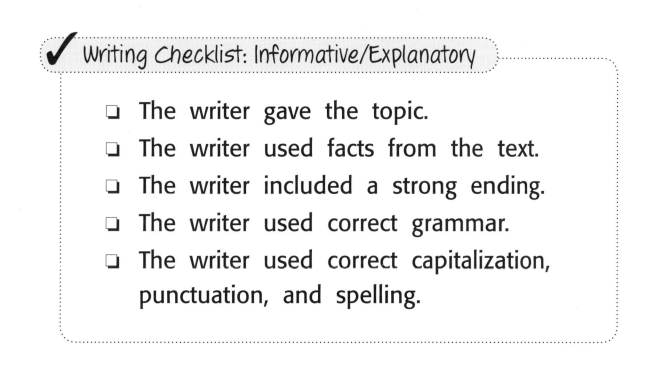

✔ Writing Checklist: Informative/Explanatory

- ❑ The writer gave the topic.
- ❑ The writer used facts from the text.
- ❑ The writer included a strong ending.
- ❑ The writer used correct grammar.
- ❑ The writer used correct capitalization, punctuation, and spelling.

COMMON CORE
STATE STANDARD

W.1.2

Writing an Informative/ Explanatory Text

Mini-Lesson 4: Respond to Informational Text

> **COMMON CORE STATE STANDARD W.1.2**
> Write informative/explanatory texts in which they name a topic, supply some facts about the topic, and provide some sense of closure.

Explain to students that they can write for the purpose of informing or explaining. Tell them that they can write informative/explanatory texts about something they have read. They might have to write information or explain something about science or social studies, a how-to passage, a biography or an autobiography, or a digital source. Then take the following steps to guide students through the process of informative/explanatory writing in response to an informational text.

Read the passage. Distribute pages 19–20 to students. Depending on students' needs, you may wish to read the passage aloud, have students read it with a partner, or have them read it independently.

Read and analyze the prompt. Read the prompt at the top of page 20 with students. Model how to analyze the prompt. Ask questions such as the following:

- *What form of writing does the writing prompt ask for?* (informative/ explanatory)

- *How can you tell?* (The prompt is asking me to explain why people like to see robins in the spring.)

- *What is the purpose of the assignment?* (to give an explanation and support it with details from the story)

- *What information do I need?* (I need to use details from the text "Robins.")

Plan the writing. Use page 20 to model how to plan writing an informative/ explanatory piece. Draw the graphic organizer on the board. As you fill in the annotations from the student model, discuss why each is appropriate. Allow students to add their own suggestions as well.

Read and analyze the model. Distribute the student writing model and checklist on page 21 to students. Read them aloud. Discuss with students whether or not the writer was successful at accomplishing the task. Ask them to complete the checklist as you discuss the informative/explanatory piece.

Read the passage below.

Robins

1. Many people like to see robins each spring. Robins are known for their red bellies. They have a nice song. Their song sounds like "cheer-up, cheer-up."

2. Robins like to hop along on grass. They look for worms to eat. Robins need water, too. They like to splash in puddles.

3. A female robin will build a nest. She will use twigs. She will use mud, too. Then she will lay eggs in the nest. A robin's eggs are blue.

4. She will sit on these eggs for many days. Then the eggs will hatch.

COMMON CORE
STATE STANDARD
W.1.2

Read and analyze the prompt.

Informative/Explanatory Writing Prompt

Why do people like to see robins in the spring? Use details from the text to support your explanation.

Plan the writing.

Main Idea:
Robins are pretty and fun to watch.
Detail 1:
They have a nice song.
Detail 2:
They hop on the grass.
Detail 3:
They splash in puddles.

Read and analyze the model.

Why People Like Robins

by Gene Ross

People think robins are pretty birds. Robins have red bellies and a cheery song. People also like that they hop on the grass. They splash in puddles. Robins lay blue eggs. People like robins in the spring.

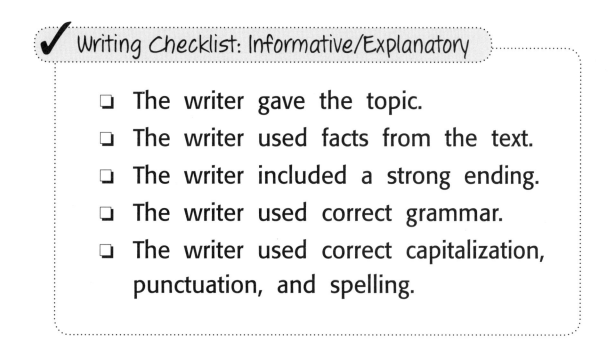

✔ Writing Checklist: Informative/Explanatory

- ❑ The writer gave the topic.
- ❑ The writer used facts from the text.
- ❑ The writer included a strong ending.
- ❑ The writer used correct grammar.
- ❑ The writer used correct capitalization, punctuation, and spelling.

COMMON CORE
STATE STANDARD
W.1.3

Writing a Narrative

Mini-Lesson 5: Respond to Literature

COMMON CORE STATE STANDARD W.1.3
Write narratives in which they recount two or more appropriately sequenced events, include some details regarding what happened, use temporal words to signal event order, and provide some sense of closure.

Explain to students that they can write a new story that includes the same characters or some details from another story. The stories they read and write may be realistic, fantasy, or may take place in the past or the future. Then take the following steps to guide students through the process of writing a narrative piece in response to literature.

Read the passage. Distribute pages 23–24 to students. Depending on students' needs, you may wish to read the passage aloud, have students read it with a partner, or have them read it independently.

Read and analyze the prompt. Read the prompt at the top of page 24 with students. Model how to analyze the prompt. Ask questions such as the following:

- *What form of writing does the writing prompt ask for?* (narrative)

- *How can you tell?* (The prompt is asking me to write a sequel to the story "The School Bus" that tells what happens next.)

- *What is the purpose of the assignment?* (to write a new story based on the details in "The School Bus")

- *What information do I need?* (I need to use details from the story "The School Bus" and my imagination.)

Plan the writing. Use page 24 to model how to plan writing a narrative. Draw the graphic organizer on the board. As you fill in the annotations from the student model, discuss why each is appropriate. Allow students to add their own suggestions as well.

Read and analyze the model. Distribute the student writing model and checklist on page 25 to students. Read them aloud. Discuss with students whether or not the writer was successful at accomplishing the task. Ask them to complete the checklist as you discuss the narrative.

COMMON CORE
STATE STANDARD
W.1.3

Read the passage below.

The School Bus

1. It was the first day of school. But Molly was not happy. She had to ride the bus. She did not want to.

2. In kindergarten, Molly walked to school. She liked this. She liked to look at the trees. She liked to listen to the birds sing.

3. She could not walk to her new school. It was too far away. She had to ride the school bus. This made her feel sad.

4. Then Molly saw her friends at the bus stop. "Hi, Molly," said Sarah.

5. "Let's all sit together," said Will. Molly felt much better.

COMMON CORE
STATE STANDARD
W.1.3

Read and analyze the prompt.

Narrative Writing Prompt

Write a new story that comes after "The School Bus." Tell what Molly, Sarah, and Will do next.

Plan the writing.

Characters:	Setting:
Molly, Sarah, and Will	the school bus

Events
They sit together on the school bus.
They have fun.
They are excited to see their new school.

Read and analyze the model.

The Ride to School

by Shona Gaines

Molly, Sarah, and Will sat together on the school bus. They talked and laughed. They had fun on the ride to school. They were very excited when they got to their new school. Molly likes the school bus now.

✔ Writing Checklist: Narrative

- ❏ The writer gave the story a title.
- ❏ The writer has events.
- ❏ The writer put the events in order.
- ❏ The writer used time words to show the order.
- ❏ The writer included a strong ending.
- ❏ The writer used correct grammar.
- ❏ The writer used correct capitalization, punctuation, and spelling.

Writing a Narrative

Mini-Lesson 6: Respond to Informational Text

> **COMMON CORE STATE STANDARD W.1.3**
> Write narratives in which they recount two or more appropriately sequenced events, include some details regarding what happened, use temporal words to signal event order, and provide some sense of closure.

Explain to students that they can write a story that includes details from a passage they have read. Tell them that the passage might be nonfiction. It might be about science or social studies, a how-to passage, a biography or an autobiography, or a digital source. Then take the following steps to guide students through the process of writing a narrative piece in response to an informational text.

Read the passage. Distribute pages 27–28 to students. Depending on students' needs, you may wish to read the passage aloud, have students read it with a partner, or have them read it independently.

Read and analyze the prompt. Read the prompt at the top of page 28 with students. Model how to analyze the prompt. Ask questions such as the following:

- *What form of writing does the writing prompt ask for?* (narrative)

- *How can you tell?* (The prompt asks me to write a story about someone who lives in the city.)

- *What is the purpose of the assignment?* (to write a narrative and support it with details from the text)

- *What information do I need?* (I need to use details from the text "City Travel" and my own imagination.)

Plan the writing. Use page 28 to model how to plan writing a narrative. Draw the graphic organizer on the board. As you fill in the annotations from the student model, discuss why each is appropriate. Allow students to add their own suggestions as well.

Read and analyze the model. Distribute the student writing model and checklist on page 29 to students. Read them aloud. Discuss with students whether or not the writer was successful at accomplishing the task. Ask them to complete the checklist as you discuss the narrative.

Read the passage below.

City Travel

1.   A city is a busy place. People in a city can travel in different ways.

2.   People like to walk from place to place. Some people drive cars. But this is not always easy. There might be traffic on city streets.

3.   Some people ride in taxicabs. Others travel on buses.

4.   A city might have trains that travel under the ground. Many people ride on these trains.

COMMON CORE
STATE STANDARD
W.1.3

Read and analyze the prompt.

Narrative Writing Prompt

Write a story about someone who lives in a city. Tell how he or she gets from place to place. Use details from the text.

Plan the writing.

Name of your characters:
Carl
Carl's mom
How your character gets from place to place:
walks
takes a taxi
rides a train

Read and analyze the model.

Carl in the Big City

by Rodney Harrison

My name is Carl. I live in a big city. Today my mom and I had to go to a store. It was too far to walk. So we got in a taxi. But then there was so much traffic! We got out and took a train. At last we got to the store.

✔ Writing Checklist: Narrative

- ❑ The writer gave the story a title.
- ❑ The writer has events.
- ❑ The writer put the events in order.
- ❑ The writer used time words to show the order.
- ❑ The writer included a strong ending.
- ❑ The writer used correct grammar.
- ❑ The writer used correct capitalization, punctuation, and spelling.

Practice Texts with Prompts

How to Use Practice Texts with Prompts

This section of *Writing to Texts* provides opportunities for students to practice writing frequently in a wide range of genres and provides authentic practice for standardized writing assessments. Each practice lesson contains a passage followed by three prompts. Below each prompt is a graphic organizer to help students plan their writing.

Before beginning, assign students one of the prompts, or ask them each to choose one. Explain to students that they are to plan and write about the passage according to the instructions in the chosen prompt. They should write on a separate sheet of paper, or in a writing journal designated for writing practice.

On pages 112–113, reproducible Student Writing Checklists are provided. Distribute them to students to serve as checklists as they write, or as self-assessment guides.

There are various ways to use the practice section. You may wish to have students complete the writing tasks at independent workstations, as homework assignments, or as test practice in a timed environment. See page 115 for ways to use the prompts for all learners at different stages of development.

Conducting Research

The Common Core State Standards require that students are provided opportunities to learn research techniques and to apply these skills in their preparation of projects.

The passages in this section can make for research project starters. After students respond to an informational prompt, guide them to conduct further research on information from the practice text in order to build their knowledge.

Explain to students that researchers take good notes, connect new knowledge to what is already known, organize information into sensible layouts for a report, cite their sources, and use their own words to convey the information.

Tell students to gather information from print and digital sources. Have them take brief notes on sources and sort their facts, details, and evidence into categories.

Practice Text with Prompts Table of Contents

COMMON CORE
STATE STANDARDS
W.1.1–
W.1.8

Name_____ Date_____

Read the passage below.

My Lost Ring
by Missy Walker

1. I looked at my hand. My ring was gone! My ring was my birthday present from Mom and Dad.

2. I looked in my bedroom. I looked in the living room. I looked in the kitchen. I could not find my ring anywhere.

3. "Mom!" I shouted. "My ring is missing."

4. "Did you look in the ring box where you keep it?" she asked.

5. I said I didn't. I was sure the ring was on my finger a few minutes ago.

6. I checked my ring box anyway. There was my ring!

7. It was not lost after all.

Common Core Writing to Texts Grade 1 • ©2014 Newmark Learning, LLC

Name_____ Date_____

Opinion/Argument Writing Prompt

Imagine it is the next day. Missy can't find her ring. Where do you think she will look for it first? Support your opinion with reasons from the text.

My Opinion:

_____

_____

_____

My Reasons:

_____

_____

_____

_____

COMMON CORE
STATE STANDARDS
W.1.1–
W.1.8

Name_____ Date_____

✏ Informative/Explanatory Writing Prompt

Why is the ring important to Missy?
Use details from the text to support
your explanation.

The ring is important to Missy because ...

_____

_____

_____

_____

_____

Name_____ Date_____

COMMON CORE
STATE STANDARDS
W.1.1–
W.1.8

Narrative Writing Prompt

Write a new story to come after "My Lost Ring." Tell what Missy does next. Tell what she does with the ring and where she goes.

Beginning:

_____

_____

Middle:

_____

_____

End:

_____

_____

COMMON CORE
STATE STANDARDS
W.1.1–
W.1.8

Name_____ Date_____

Read the passage below.

Luke's Problem

1. Luke got into his spaceship. He pressed the button that said "school." His spaceship rose into the air. Then it went to Luke's school.

2. Luke liked living on the moon. He liked walking in moon dust. He liked playing with moon rocks. He liked his school.

3. But Luke had a problem. He really wanted to see Earth.

4. He wanted to see grass. He wanted to hear birds sing. He thought it would be fun to climb a tree.

5. He hoped his parents would take him there one day. It would be a very special vacation.

Opinion/Argument Writing Prompt

Do you think the moon in this story is a good place to live? Support your opinion with details from the text.

My Opinion:

_____

_____

_____

My Reasons:

_____

_____

_____

COMMON CORE
STATE STANDARDS
W.1.1–
W.1.8

Name_____ Date_____

Informative/Explanatory Writing Prompt

Why does Luke want to see Earth? Use details from the text to support your explanation.

Luke wants to see Earth because . . . _____

_____

_____

_____

_____

_____

Name_____ Date_____

Narrative Writing Prompt

Write a story in which Luke visits Earth. What does he see there? What does he do? Use details from the text in your story.

What Luke Sees:

_____

_____

_____

What Luke Does:

_____

_____

_____

COMMON CORE
STATE STANDARDS
W.1.1–
W.1.8

Name_____ Date_____

Read the passage below.

The Camping Trip

1.   Ben and his family were going camping. Ben was excited. They drove to the campground. They found a nice spot.

2.   Then they put up two tents. Ben and his brother Matt had their own tent.

3.   Ben's parents built a fire. They cooked food over the fire. It tasted good. Ben was having fun.

4.   But at night they heard thunder. Then it started to rain. Ben and Matt packed up their tent. Mom and Dad packed up their tent, too.

5.   Then they all ran to the car. Ben laughed. They were going home!

  Common Core Writing to Texts Grade 1 • ©2014 Newmark Learning, LLC

Name_____ Date_____

COMMON CORE
STATE STANDARDS
W.1.1–
W.1.8

Opinion/Argument Writing Prompt

Do you think it would be fun to go with Ben and his family on this camping trip? Why or why not? Use details from the text.

My Opinion:

_____

_____

_____

My Reasons:

_____

_____

_____

COMMON CORE
STATE STANDARDS
W.1.1–
W.1.8

Name_____ Date_____

Informative/Explanatory Writing Prompt

What do Ben and his family do when it starts to rain? Use details from the text to support your explanation.

When it starts to rain, Ben and his family ... _____

_____

_____

_____

_____

Common Core Writing to Texts Grade 1 • ©2014 Newmark Learning, LLC

Name_____ Date_____

COMMON CORE
STATE STANDARDS
W.1.1–
W.1.8

Narrative Writing Prompt

Write a story in which you go camping. Use words such as *I* and *me* to tell what happens and how you feel. Use details from the text.

Beginning:

_____

_____

Middle:

_____

_____

End:

_____

_____

COMMON CORE
STATE STANDARDS
W.1.1–
W.1.8

Name_____ Date_____

Read the passage below.

Jack and the Beanstalk

1. Once upon a time, there was a boy named Jack. Jack lived with his mother. They were very poor.

2. Jack traded his family's cow for some beans. This upset his mother. She threw the beans out the window.

3. The beans grew into a giant beanstalk! Jack climbed it. A big house was at the top. A giant lived in this house. This giant was mean to children.

4. Jack knocked on the door. He asked the giant's wife for a glass of milk. She told him to come in. She gave him the milk.

5. Jack saw many bags of gold on the floor. *This gold belongs to the mean giant*, he thought.

6. Then he heard the giant's footsteps. He grabbed a bag of gold. Then he went down the beanstalk. He gave the gold to his mother. She was very happy.

Name_____ Date_____

COMMON CORE
STATE STANDARDS
W.1.1–
W.1.8

Opinion/Argument Writing Prompt

Do you think it was okay for Jack to take a bag of gold from the giant's house? Why or why not? Support your opinion with reasons from the text.

My Opinion:

_____

_____

_____

My Reasons:

_____

_____

_____

_____

COMMON CORE
STATE STANDARDS
W.1.1–
W.1.8

Name_____ Date_____

Informative/Explanatory Writing Prompt

What can you tell about the giant's wife from the story? Use details from the story to support your explanation.

The giant's wife is _____ because she

_____

_____

_____

_____

_____

_____

Common Core Writing to Texts Grade 1 • ©2014 Newmark Learning, LLC

Name_____ Date_____

COMMON CORE
STATE STANDARDS
W.1.1–
W.1.8

Narrative Writing Prompt

Write what Jack and his mother will say to each other when Jack comes home with the bag of gold.

Jack:

_____

_____

Mother:

_____

_____

Jack:

_____

_____

Mother:

_____

_____

COMMON CORE
STATE STANDARDS
W.1.1–
W.1.8

Name_____ Date_____

Read the passage below.

Why Rabbit Has a Short Tail

1. A long time ago, Rabbit had a long, furry tail. Rabbit liked to show others her tail.

2. "It is the most beautiful tail in the world," she said.

3. Fox was tired of this. He wanted to teach Rabbit a lesson. Fox cut a hole in the ice. He put his tail in the hole. He told Rabbit he was going to catch a fish. The fish would grab onto his tail.

4. Rabbit liked to eat fish. Rabbit stuck her tail in the hole.

5. "Keep it in there for a long time," Fox said. "A fish will come along."

6. Rabbit kept her tail in the hole all night. It froze. When she stood, it broke off.

7. This is why a rabbit has a short tail.

Name_____ Date_____

COMMON CORE
STATE STANDARDS
W.1.1–
W.1.8

Opinion/Argument Writing Prompt

Do you think Fox is unkind in this story? Why or why not? Support your opinion with details from the text.

My Opinion:

_____

_____

_____

My Reasons:

_____

_____

_____

COMMON CORE
STATE STANDARDS
W.1.1–
W.1.8

Name_____ Date_____

Informative/Explanatory Writing Prompt

Why does Fox put his tail in a hole in the ice? Support your explanation with details from the text.

Fox put his tail in the ice because . . . _____

_____

_____

_____

_____

Common Core Writing to Texts Grade 1 • ©2014 Newmark Learning, LLC

Name_____ Date_____

Narrative Writing Prompt

Rewrite the story from Rabbit's point of view. Use words such as *I* and *me* to describe what happens and how you feel.

Beginning:

_____

_____

Middle:

_____

_____

End:

_____

_____

Common Core
State Standards
W.1.1–
W.1.8

Name_____ Date_____

Read the passage below.

Coco's Bath

1. Beth and Maggie played with their dog in their yard. Her name was Coco.

2. They threw Coco a ball. Coco brought the ball back. They ran in a big circle. Coco ran, too.

3. Then they jumped over a mud puddle. But Coco jumped in the puddle. Coco was covered in mud.

4. Beth and Maggie took Coco in the house. They put her in the tub. They wet her fur. They covered her fur with shampoo. Then they rinsed her fur.

5. Coco was clean. But Beth and Maggie were muddy and wet!

Common Core Writing to Texts Grade 1 • ©2014 Newmark Learning, LLC

Name_____ Date_____

COMMON CORE STATE STANDARDS

W.1.1– W.1.8

Opinion/Argument Writing Prompt

Do you think it would be fun to give a dog a bath? Support your opinion with details from the text.

Opinion:

Reasons:

COMMON CORE
STATE STANDARDS
W.1.1–
W.1.8

Name_____ Date_____

Informative/Explanatory Writing Prompt

Why do Beth and Maggie give Coco a bath? Support your explanation with details from the text.

Beth and Maggie give Coco a bath because . . ._____

_____

_____

_____

_____

_____

Common Core Writing to Texts Grade 1 • ©2014 Newmark Learning, LLC

Name_____ Date_____

Narrative Writing Prompt

Write a journal entry Beth might have recorded after her "Coco's Bath" adventure.

Date _____

_____

_____

_____

_____

_____

_____

COMMON CORE
STATE STANDARDS
W.1.1–
W.1.8

Name_____ Date_____

Read the passage below.

Baby's Birthday

1. A baby had a basket

2. and a little red balloon.

3. She got them for her birthday

4. On a sunny day in June.

5. A dolly in a pretty dress

6. Was sitting in the store.

7. Baby came to buy her

8. And she walked her out the door.

9. Baby had a happy day.

10. A hat was on her head.

11. She had a party in the yard

12. And then she went to bed.

Name_____ Date_____

COMMON CORE
STATE STANDARDS
W.1.1–
W.1.8

Opinion/Argument Writing Prompt

How do you think the baby felt
when she went to bed? Why?
Use details from the poem to explain
your opinion.

My Opinion:

_____

_____

My Reasons:

_____

_____

_____

_____

COMMON CORE
STATE STANDARDS
W.1.1–
W.1.8

Name_____ Date_____

Informative/Explanatory Writing Prompt

What does the baby get for her birthday? Support your explanations with details from the poem.

For her birthday, the baby gets ...

_____

_____

_____

_____

_____

_____

Common Core Writing to Texts Grade 1 • ©2014 Newmark Learning, LLC

Name_____ Date_____

COMMON CORE
STATE STANDARDS
W.1.1–
W.1.8

Narrative Writing Prompt

Rewrite the poem as a story from the baby's point of view. Give your story a beginning, a middle, and an end.

Beginning:

_____

_____

Middle:

_____

_____

End:

_____

_____

COMMON CORE
STATE STANDARDS
W.1.1–
W.1.8

Name_____ Date_____

Read the passage below.

Missed the Bus

1. I was very tired this morning. I slept too long. I missed my bus. I heard it drive by my house. But I was still in bed.

2. There was going to be a spelling quiz! But I would be late for school. I was going to miss the quiz.

3. "I need help!" I yelled to Dad. "I'm going to be late for school."

4. "Relax, Eric," Dad said. "I can give you a ride."

5. "Thanks, Dad," I said. I wasn't going to miss my spelling quiz after all.

Name_____ Date_____

COMMON CORE
STATE STANDARDS
W.1.1–
W.1.8

Opinion/Argument Writing Prompt

Do you think Dad should have helped Eric? Why or why not? Support your opinion with details from the text.

My Opinion:

_____

_____

My Reasons:

_____

_____

_____

_____

COMMON CORE
STATE STANDARDS
W.1.1–
W.1.8

Name_____ Date_____

Informative/Explanatory Writing Prompt

Why does Eric miss the bus? Use details from the text to support your explanation.

Eric misses the bus because ...

Common Core Writing to Texts Grade 1 • ©2014 Newmark Learning, LLC

Name_____ Date_____

COMMON CORE
STATE STANDARDS
W.1.1–
W.1.8

Narrative Writing Prompt

Write a new story to come after "Missed the Bus." Tell what happens next.

First:

_____

_____

Next:

_____

_____

Last:

_____

_____

Common Core
State Standards
W.1.1–
W.1.8

Name_____ Date_____

Read the passage below.

The Baby Bird

1. Rick was playing ball outside. He threw the ball to his friend Evan. Evan threw the ball back.

2. Rick heard a strange noise. It sounded like a bird.

3. Rick looked around. He saw a baby bird in the grass.

4. "What should we do?" he asked Evan. "I think it fell out of its nest."

5. Evan looked high in a bush. "I see the nest!" he said. He saw more baby birds in the nest. "Let's put it back in the nest."

6. Rick carefully picked up the baby bird. He carefully put it in the nest. Then Rick and Evan walked away.

7. The mother bird flew to the nest and fed the babies.

Name_____ Date_____

Opinion/Argument Writing Prompt

Do you think it is a good idea for Rick and Evan to put a baby bird back in a nest? Why or why not? Support your opinion with details from the text.

My Opinion:

_____

_____

My Reasons:

_____

_____

_____

_____

COMMON CORE
STATE STANDARDS
W.1.1–
W.1.8

Name_____ Date_____

Informative/Explanatory Writing Prompt

What can you tell about Rick and Evan from the story? Use details from the text to support your explanation.

Rick and Evan are _____ because they _____

_____

_____

_____

_____

_____

COMMON CORE
STATE STANDARDS
W.1.1–
W.1.8

Name_____ Date_____

Narrative Writing Prompt

Rewrite the story from the baby bird's point of view. Use words such as *I* and *me* to describe what happens and how you feel.

Beginning:

_____

_____

Middle:

_____

_____

End:

_____

_____

Common Core State Standards
W.1.1–
W.1.8

Name_____ Date_____

Read the passage below.

The New Fish

1. **Narrator:** Yellow Fish, Purple Fish, and Crab live together. They are happy. Then one day, Big Fish comes there. They are afraid of her.

2. **Yellow Fish:** What should we do? Do you think she is here to eat us?

3. **Purple Fish:** We should ask her why she is here. But I am too scared.

4. **Yellow Fish:** So am I! I am afraid to talk to her.

5. **Crab:** I'll talk to her. I'm not afraid.

6. **Big Fish:** Hi! Do you want to be my friend?

7. **Crab:** Are you going to eat my friends and me?

8. **Big Fish:** No! I just moved here. But I need some friends.

9. **Crab:** We'll be your friends!

10. **Narrator:** Crab takes Big Fish to meet Yellow Fish and Purple Fish.

COMMON CORE
STATE STANDARDS
W.1.1–
W.1.8

Name_____ Date_____

Opinion/Argument Writing Prompt

Do you think Crab is brave or foolish? Support your opinion with details from the play.

My Opinion:

_____

_____

My Reasons:

_____

_____

_____

COMMON CORE
STATE STANDARDS
W.1.1–
W.1.8

Name_____ Date_____

Informative/Explanatory Writing Prompt

Why are Yellow Fish and Purple Fish afraid to talk to Big Fish? Use details from the play to support your explanation.

Yellow Fish and Purple Fish are afraid to talk to Big

Fish because ...

_____

_____

_____

_____

_____

_____

Name_____ Date_____

COMMON CORE
STATE STANDARDS
**W.1.1–
W.1.8**

Narrative Writing Prompt

Write a story that comes after the play. Tell what happens when Big Fish meets Yellow Fish and Purple Fish.

Beginning:

_____

_____

Middle:

_____

_____

End:

_____

_____

Common Core State Standards
W.1.1–
W.1.8

Name_____ Date_____

Read the passage below.

Rain Forests

1. A rain forest is a beautiful place. It has giant trees. It has many plants.

2. Many animals live in a rain forest. Monkeys swing in trees. Colorful birds sing songs. Frogs live there, too. Many snakes live in a rain forest. You might even see a giant butterfly there.

3. Some rain forests have large rivers. Many fish live in these rivers.

4. It is very hot in a rain forest. And it might rain every day. Most rain forests are near the center of Earth. This is the hottest place on Earth.

Common Core Writing to Texts Grade 1 • ©2014 Newmark Learning, LLC

Name_____ Date_____

COMMON CORE
STATE STANDARDS
W.1.1–
W.1.8

Opinion/Argument Writing Prompt

Do you think a rain forest is a good place to visit? Why or why not? Support your opinion with reasons from the text.

My Opinion:

_____

_____

My Reasons:

_____

_____

_____

_____

COMMON CORE
STATE STANDARDS

W.1.1–
W.1.8

Name_____ Date_____

Informative/Explanatory Writing Prompt

What are some animals that live in a rain forest? Support your explanation with details from the text.

Animals That Live in a Rain Forest

_____

_____

_____

_____

_____

_____

Name_____ Date_____

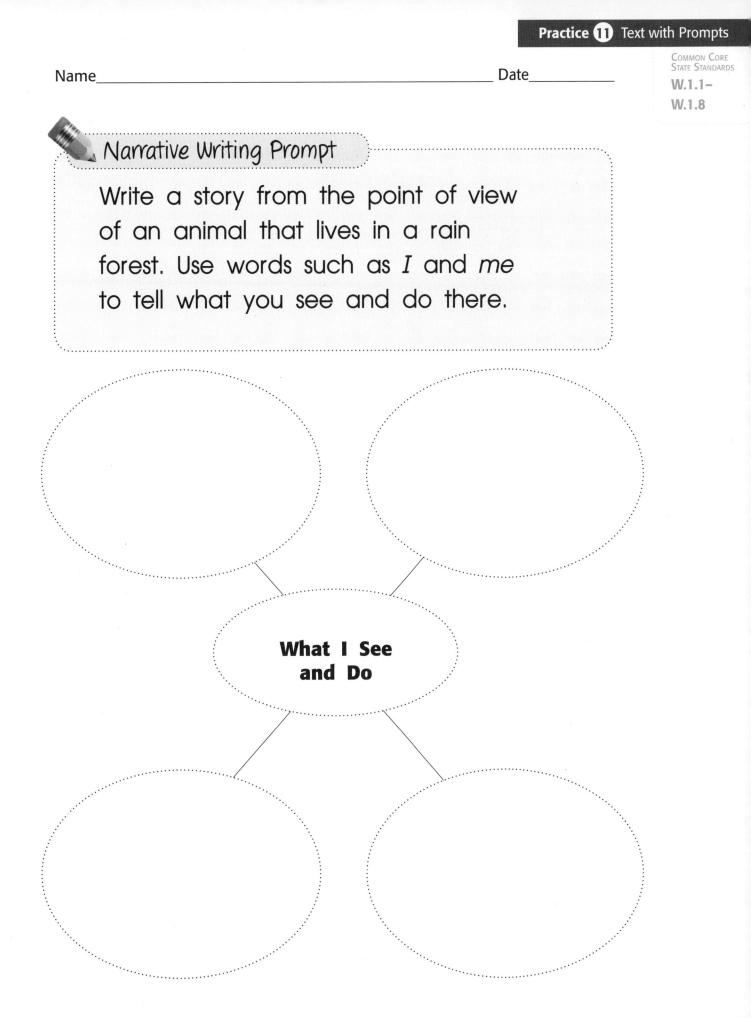

Narrative Writing Prompt

Write a story from the point of view of an animal that lives in a rain forest. Use words such as *I* and *me* to tell what you see and do there.

What I See and Do

COMMON CORE
STATE STANDARDS
W.1.1–
W.1.8

Name_____ Date_____

Read the passage below.

Dolphins

1. A dolphin looks like a big fish. It can stay under the water for a long time. But a dolphin needs air. It has a hole on the top of its head. It breathes through this hole.

2. People see dolphins when they come out of the water for air.

3. Dolphins like people. They sometimes swim up to people.

4. Dolphins live together in groups. About ten dolphins are in a group.

5. A dolphin always looks happy. Its mouth turns up at the ends. A dolphin looks like it is smiling!

Name_____ Date_____

COMMON CORE
STATE STANDARDS
W.1.1–
W.1.8

Opinion/Argument Writing Prompt

How would you describe, or tell about, a dolphin? Support your opinion with details from the text.

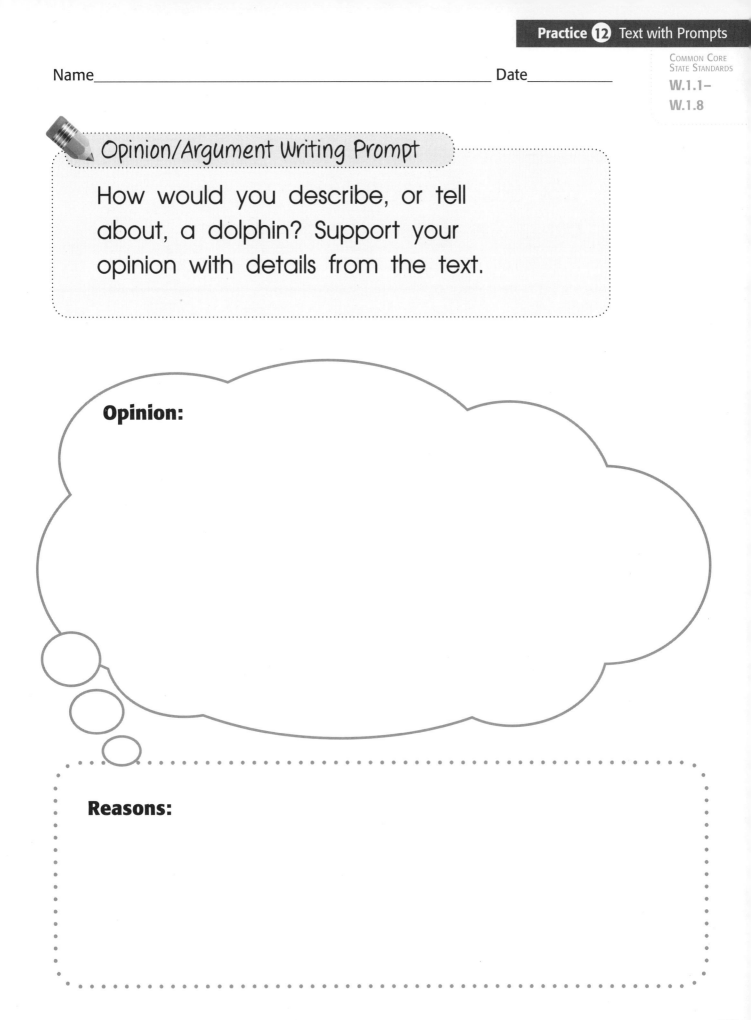

Opinion:

Reasons:

COMMON CORE
STATE STANDARDS
W.1.1–
W.1.8

Name_____ Date_____

Informative/Explanatory Writing Prompt

Why does a dolphin have to come out of the water? Use details from the text to support your explanation.

A dolphin has to come out of the water because ...

Common Core Writing to Texts Grade 1 • ©2014 Newmark Learning, LLC

Name_____ Date_____

COMMON CORE
STATE STANDARDS
W.1.1–
W.1.8

Narrative Writing Prompt

Imagine that you have just seen a group of dolphins. Write a journal entry you might record about it. Use details from the text.

Date _____

_____

_____

_____

_____

_____

COMMON CORE
STATE STANDARDS
W.1.1–
W.1.8

Name_____ Date_____

Read the passage below.

Maps

1. A map is a drawing of a place. A map can help you go from one place to another place.

2. What if you want to go to the library? You could look at a map of your town. It might show you what streets to take. It might help you get to the library.

3. A map can show you how far away a place is.

4. A map might have pictures on it. Each picture might mean something. A picture of an airplane might mean an airport.

5. Maps are very helpful. We might get lost without them.

COMMON CORE
STATE STANDARDS
W.1.1–
W.1.8

Name_____ Date_____

Opinion/Argument Writing Prompt

The text says, "Maps are very helpful."
Do you agree? Why or why not?
Support your opinion with details from
the text.

My Opinion:

_____

_____

My Reasons:

_____

_____

_____

_____

COMMON CORE
STATE STANDARDS
W.1.1–
W.1.8

Name_____ Date_____

Informative/Explanatory Writing Prompt

What are some ways that a map could help you? Support your explanation with details from the text.

Ways a Map Can Help You

_____

_____

_____

_____

_____

_____

Name_____ Date_____

COMMON CORE
STATE STANDARDS
W.1.1–
W.1.8

Narrative Writing Prompt

Write a story about a kid that uses a map to get somewhere. Use details from the text in your story.

Beginning:

_____

_____

Middle:

_____

_____

End:

_____

_____

COMMON CORE
STATE STANDARDS
W.1.1–
W.1.8

Name_____ Date_____

Read the passage below.

Center Street School News

FEBRUARY 28

The Talent Show

by Kim Brown

1. Our school will hold a Talent Show on Friday. It will start at 6:00. It will take place in the gym.

2. Many students will be in the Talent Show. Some will sing. Others will dance. Some will make music. One student will do magic tricks. Another will read a poem. Some students will try to make us laugh. All students will get a prize for their hard work.

3. You need a ticket to go to the Talent Show. Tickets cost $2.00. You can buy them in the school office.

COMMON CORE
STATE STANDARDS
W.1.1–
W.1.8

Name_____ Date_____

Opinion/Argument Writing Prompt

Would you like to be in a Talent Show at your school? Why or why not? Support your opinion with details from the text.

My Opinion:

_____

_____

My Reasons:

_____

_____

_____

_____

COMMON CORE
STATE STANDARDS
W.1.1–
W.1.8

Name_____ Date_____

✏️ Informative/Explanatory Writing Prompt

Imagine that you want to watch the Talent Show at this school. What would you have to do? Use details from the text in your explanation.

To go to the Talent Show, I would have to . . .

_____

_____

_____

_____

_____

_____

Name_____ Date_____

COMMON CORE
STATE STANDARD
W.1.1–
W.1.8

Narrative Writing Prompt

Write a journal entry a student might write after being in the Talent Show.

Date _____

_____

_____

_____

_____

_____

COMMON CORE
STATE STANDARDS
W.1.1–
W.1.8

Name_____ Date_____

Read the passage below.

How to Care for an Ant Farm

1. An ant farm is a fun way to learn about ants. Do not try to make your own ant farm.

2. **Step 1:** With an adult, buy an ant farm kit at a store or online.

3. **Step 2:** Place the ants into the ant farm. Be careful! Make sure they cannot get out.

4. **Step 3:** Put food and water into the farm.

5. **Step 4:** Keep your ant farm in the shade. They do not like being too hot or too cold.

6. Now you can enjoy your tiny pets! Watch the ants. You can use a hand lens.

7. Watch how the ants dig tunnels. Notice how they have different jobs.

8. You will see that ants are hard workers and very clean.

Common Core Writing to Texts Grade 1 • ©2014 Newmark Learning, LLC

Name_____ Date_____

COMMON CORE
STATE STANDARDS
W.1.1–
W.1.8

Opinion/Argument Writing Prompt

Do you think ants make good pets? Why or why not? Support your opinion with details from the text.

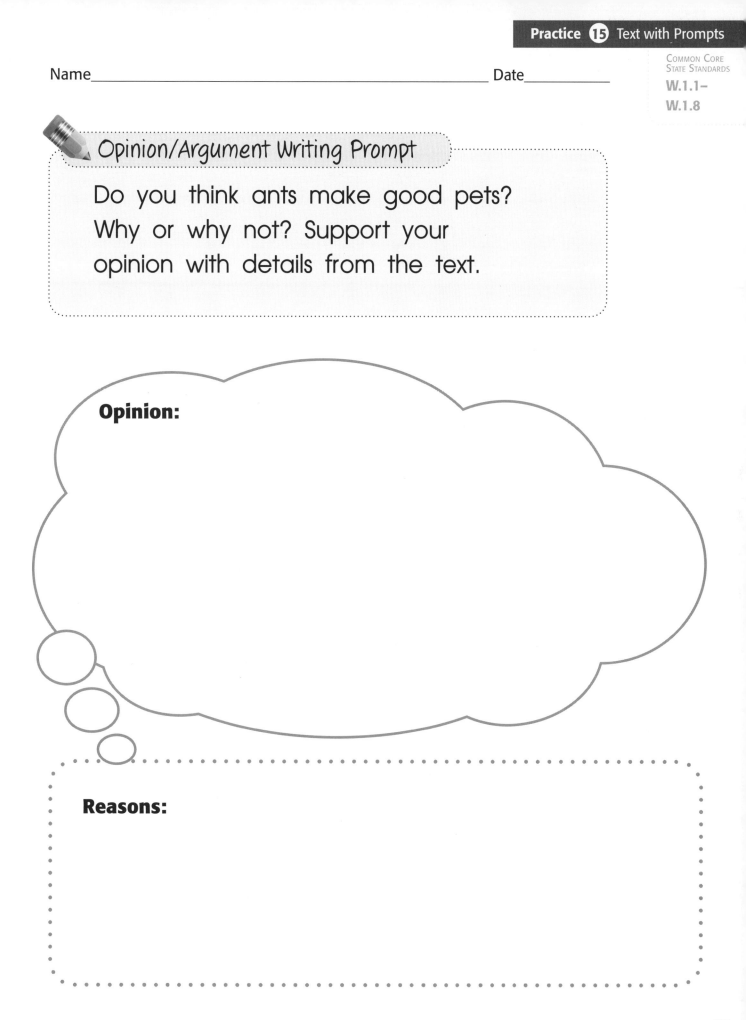

Opinion:

Reasons:

COMMON CORE
STATE STANDARDS
W.1.1–
W.1.8

Name_____ Date_____

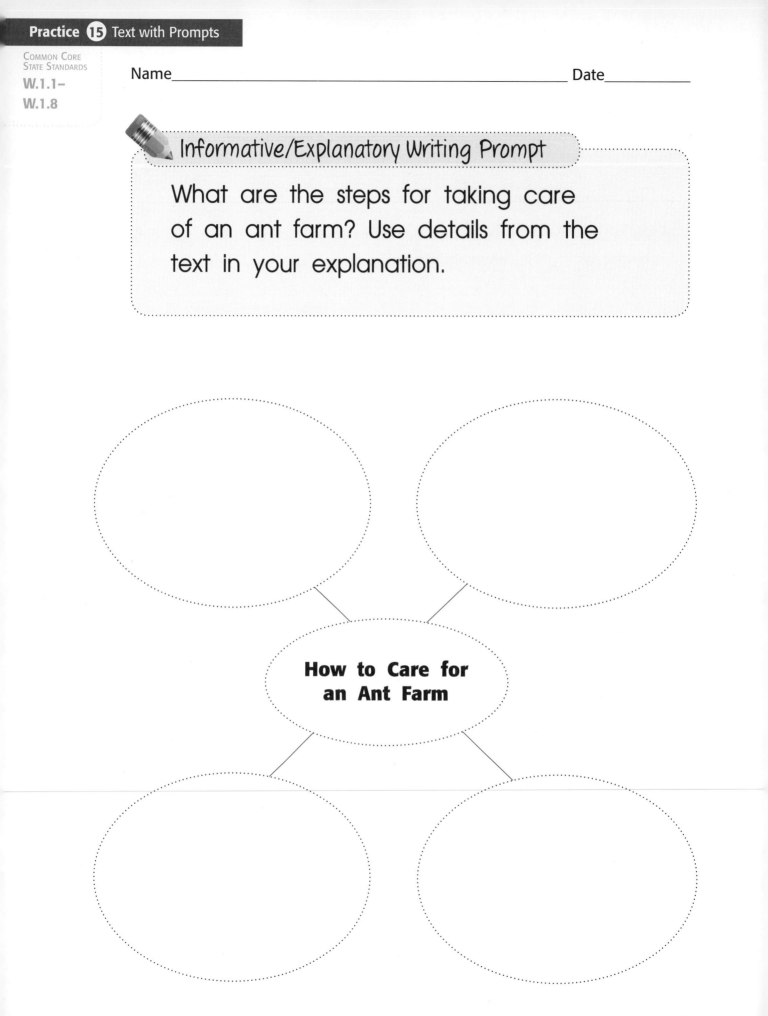

Informative/Explanatory Writing Prompt

What are the steps for taking care of an ant farm? Use details from the text in your explanation.

How to Care for an Ant Farm

Common Core Writing to Texts Grade 1 • ©2014 Newmark Learning, LLC

Name_____ Date_____

Narrative Writing Prompt

Write a story from the point of view of a boy or a girl who has an ant farm. Use words such as *I* and *me* to describe what you do and how you feel.

Beginning:

_____

_____

Middle:

_____

_____

End:

_____

_____

COMMON CORE
STATE STANDARDS
W.1.1–
W.1.8

Name_____ Date_____

Read the passage below.

Desert

1. A desert is a place that is very dry. Many deserts are hot places. But some are cold places.

2. Some plants grow in deserts. These plants do not need much water.

3. Some animals live in deserts. These animals do not need much water. Some do not drink water. They get water from their food.

4. Most desert animals sleep during the day. They are awake at night. It is cooler in a desert at night.

5. Most deserts have lots of sand. But some also have rocks and mountains. Not many people live in deserts.

 Common Core Writing to Texts Grade 1 • ©2014 Newmark Learning, LLC

Name_____ Date_____

COMMON CORE
STATE STANDARDS
W.1.1–
W.1.8

Opinion/Argument Writing Prompt

Do you think a desert is a good place for people to live? Support your opinion with details from the text.

My Opinion:

_____

_____

My Reasons:

_____

_____

_____

_____

COMMON CORE
STATE STANDARDS
W.1.1–
W.1.8

Name_____ Date_____

Informative/Explanatory Writing Prompt

What do you know about animals that live in a desert? Use details from the text to support your explanation.

Animals that live in a desert...

_____

_____

_____

_____

_____

_____

Name_____ Date_____

COMMON CORE
STATE STANDARDS
W.1.1–
W.1.8

Narrative Writing Prompt

Write a story from the point of view of an animal that lives in a desert such as a fox or a mouse. Use words such as *I* and *me* to tell what you do and how you feel.

What I Do: _____

_____

_____

_____

How I Feel: _____

_____

_____

_____

COMMON CORE
STATE STANDARDS
W.1.1–
W.1.8

Name_____ Date_____

Read the passage below.

Helen Keller

1. Helen Keller was a very special person. Helen became sick when she was very young.

2. After this, she could not see. She could not hear, either. Helen could not talk to people. She could not hear them talk to her.

3. Later, Helen had a special teacher. Her name was Annie. Annie taught Helen words. She drew letters with her fingers in Helen's hand. Helen learned to spell words.

4. Annie taught Helen how to read special books. These books are for blind people.

5. Later, Helen learned how to talk, too. She was much happier after this.

COMMON CORE
STATE STANDARDS
W.1.1–
W.1.8

Name_____ Date_____

Opinion/Argument Writing Prompt

Do you think Annie was a good teacher? Why or why not? Support your opinion with details from the text.

My Opinion:

_____

_____

My Reasons:

_____

_____

_____

COMMON CORE
STATE STANDARDS
W.1.1–
W.1.8

Name_____ Date_____

Informative/Explanatory Writing Prompt

How did Helen learn to spell words? Use details from the text to support your explanation.

Helen learned to spell words . . . _____

_____

_____

_____

_____

Common Core Writing to Texts Grade 1 • ©2014 Newmark Learning, LLC

Name_____ Date_____

COMMON CORE
STATE STANDARDS
W.1.1–
W.1.8

Narrative Writing Prompt

Write a story from Annie's point of view. Tell how you teach Helen to spell words. Use words such as *I* and *me* to describe what happens and how you feel.

What I Do: _____

_____

_____

_____

How I Feel: _____

_____

_____

_____

COMMON CORE
STATE STANDARDS
W.1.1–
W.1.8

Name_____ Date_____

Read the passage below.

The Sun

1. The sun is a giant star. It is made of gas and dust. It is like a big ball of fire.

2. The sun gives us light. It also gives us heat. Earth would be frozen without the sun.

3. The sun is huge. It is much bigger than Earth. The sun looks like it is very close to Earth. This is because the sun is so big. But the sun is very far away.

4. The sun does not move. But Earth moves around the sun.

COMMON CORE
STATE STANDARDS
W.1.1–
W.1.8

Name_____ Date_____

Opinion/Argument Writing Prompt

Do you think the sun is important to people on Earth? Why or why not? Support your opinion with details from the text.

My Opinion:

_____

_____

My Reasons:

_____

_____

_____

_____

COMMON CORE
STATE STANDARDS
W.1.1–
W.1.8

Name_____ Date_____

Informative/Explanatory Writing Prompt

Why does the sun look like it is close to Earth? Support your explanation with details from the text.

The sun looks like it's close to Earth because ...

_____

_____

_____

_____

102

Name_____ Date_____

COMMON CORE
STATE STANDARDS
W.1.1–
W.1.8

Narrative Writing Prompt

Imagine that the sun can talk. Write a story from the sun's point of view. Tell what you do to help Earth.

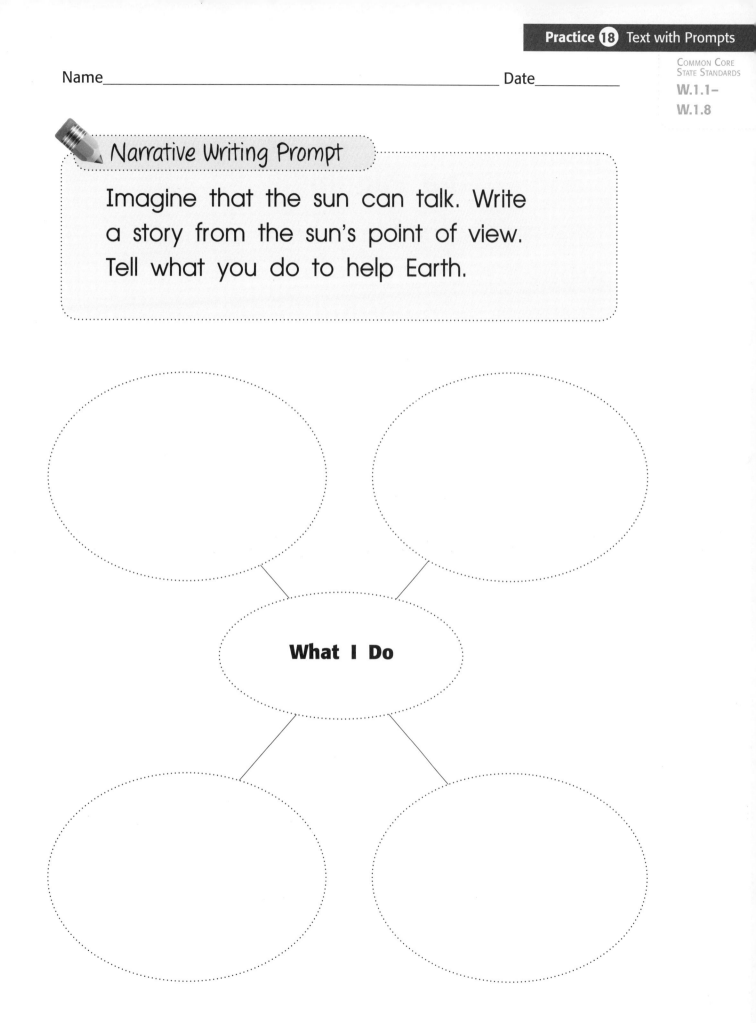

What I Do

COMMON CORE
STATE STANDARDS
W.1.1–
W.1.8

Name_____ Date_____

Read the passage below.

The Pilgrims

1. The Pilgrims lived in another country. They came to America to be free.

2. Some of them came on the *Mayflower*. This was a large ship.

3. The Pilgrims were very poor. They did not know how to grow food. They did not have enough food to eat.

4. The Native Americans helped them. They taught the Pilgrims to grow food. They taught them to grow corn and peas.

5. The Pilgrims and the Native Americans ate a special meal together.

6. This was the first Thanksgiving.

Name_____ Date_____

Opinion/Argument Writing Prompt

Why do you think the Native
Americans helped the Pilgrims?
Support your opinion with details
from the text.

My Opinion:

_____

_____

My Reasons:

_____

_____

_____

_____

COMMON CORE
STATE STANDARDS
W.1.1–
W.1.8

Name_____ Date_____

Informative/Explanatory Writing Prompt

Why didn't the Pilgrims have enough food to eat? Support your explanation with details from the text.

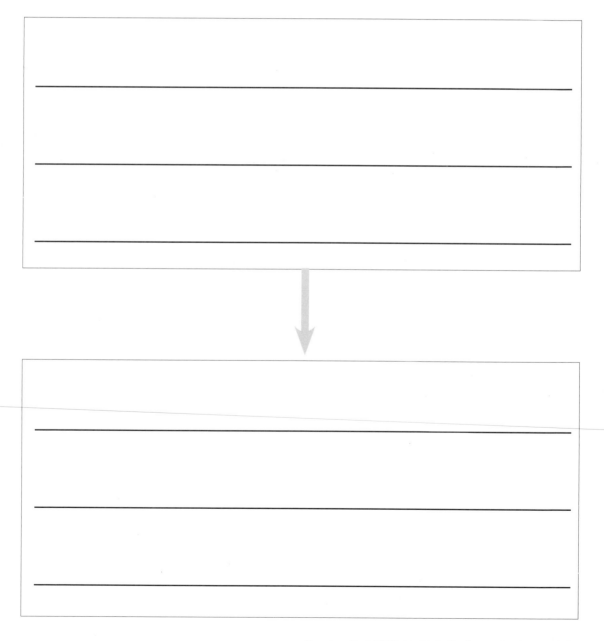

Name_____ Date_____

COMMON CORE
STATE STANDARDS
W.1.1–
W.1.8

Narrative Writing Prompt

Write a story from the point of view of a Pilgrim who was at the first Thanksgiving. Give your character a name and include what people say in your story.

Beginning:

_____

_____

Middle:

_____

_____

End:

_____

_____

COMMON CORE
STATE STANDARDS
W.1.1–
W.1.8

Name_____ Date_____

Read the passage below.

Get Moving!

1.   Kids need exercise. You should exercise every day.

2.   Exercise is good for your body. It keeps your heart strong. It makes you feel good, too. You will be happier if you exercise.

3.   You can exercise in different ways. You can play on the swings at a park. You can swing on monkey bars. You can jump rope. These are great ways to exercise.

4.   You can also play games. You can play basketball. You can play soccer. You can ride your bike to exercise. You can roller-skate.

5.   The important thing is to move—and to have fun!

Common Core Writing to Texts Grade 1 • ©2014 Newmark Learning, LLC

Name_____ Date_____

COMMON CORE
STATE STANDARDS
W.1.1–
W.1.8

Opinion/Argument Writing Prompt

Do you think it's important to exercise? Why or why not? Support your opinion with details from the text.

My Opinion:

_____

_____

My Reasons:

_____

_____

_____

COMMON CORE
STATE STANDARDS
W.1.1–
W.1.8

Name_____ Date_____

Informative/Explanatory Writing Prompt

What are some ways that kids can get exercise? Use details from the text and your own ideas to support your explanation.

Ways Kids Can Get Exercise

_____

_____

_____

_____

_____

_____

_____

Name_____ Date_____

Narrative Writing Prompt

Write a story about three kids who decide to get more exercise. Give your characters names and tell what they do.

Beginning:

_____

_____

Middle:

_____

_____

End:

_____

_____

COMMON CORE
STATE STANDARDS
W.1.1–
W.1.3,
W.1.5

Name_____ Date_____

✔ Writing Checklist: Opinion/Argument

❏ I gave the title of the text.

❏ I gave the topic.

❏ I stated an opinion.

❏ I gave reasons to support my opinion.

❏ I included a strong ending.

❏ I used correct grammar.

❏ I used correct capitalization, punctuation, and spelling.

✔ Writing Checklist: Informative/Explanatory

❏ I gave the topic.

❏ I used facts from the text.

❏ I included a strong ending.

❏ I used correct grammar.

❏ I used correct capitalization, punctuation, and spelling.

COMMON CORE
STATE STANDARDS
W.1.1–
W.1.3,
W.1.5

Name_____ Date_____

✔ Writing Checklist: Narrative

❏ I gave my story a title.

❏ I have events.

❏ I put the events in order.

❏ I used time words to show the order.

❏ I included a strong ending.

❏ I used correct grammar.

❏ I used correct capitalization, punctuation, and spelling.

Rubrics and Assessments

Using the Rubrics to Assess Students and Differentiate Instruction

This section contains tools to help you assess students and guide them to become strong writers. On page 115, refer to the chart for suggestions of how to use text-based writing prompts with all learners.

Pages 116–117 provides an Observational Writing Assessment Checklist to help document students' progress throughout the year.

Use the Evaluation Rubrics on page 119 to guide your assessment of students' responses. The rubrics are based on the Common Core State Standards for writing. Similar rubrics will be used by evaluators to score new standardized assessments.

After scoring students' writing, refer to the differentiated rubrics on pages 120–125. These are designed to help you differentiate your interactions and instruction to match students' needs. For each score a student receives in the Evaluation Rubrics, responsive prompts are provided to support writers. These gradual-release prompts scaffold writers toward mastery of each writing type.

• For a score of 1, use the Goal Oriented prompts.

• For a score of 2, use the Directive and Corrective Feedback prompts.

• For a score of 3, use the Self-Monitoring and Reflection prompts.

• For a score of 4, use the Validating and Confirming prompts.

Using Technology

If you choose to have students use computers to write and revise their work, consider these ways to support online collaboration and digital publishing:

• Google Drive facilitates collaboration and allows teachers and peers to provide real-time feedback on writing pieces.

• Wikis enable students to share their writing around a common topic.

• Audio tools enable students to record their works (podcasts) for others to hear on a safe sharing platform.

• Student writing can be enriched with images, audio, and video.

Ways to Use the Prompts	Description
Oral Language Development	Work with students to respond to the prompts orally. Model academic language structures students need to provide a complete response. Help students locate information in the text that supports their ideas. Encourage students to expand on their ideas. With beginning English learners, transfer speaking to writing by dictating some of their ideas on paper and rereading them together. With students able to write in English, this activity can be an oral rehearsal for their independent writing.
Modeling or Shared Writing Lessons	With beginning and/or struggling writers, model how you think about what a writing prompt is asking you to do, and compose a message by drawing and/or writing. Depending on the developmental writing stage students are in, use the opportunity to model how you: • Rehearse your ideas orally. • Draw on evidence from the text. • Use drawing to help you get started. • Apply concepts about print. • Apply phonetic knowledge to write unknown words. • Hear and write familiar sight words. • Use a writing checklist to help you structure your opinion, informative, or narrative writing piece. • Check your grammar and conventions.
Interactive Writing Lessons	Work collaboratively with students to orally construct a response to a prompt and write it. Allow students to share the pen and write as much of the response as they can. Support students based on their needs.
Partner Writing	Allow struggling writers to collaborate with a peer to write a response to a prompt. Encourage them to orally rehearse their ideas before they write. Confer with students to ensure that they are addressing the prompt and using evidence from the text.
Independent Writing	With students who are able to write independently, allow them to respond to the prompts during small-group independent workstation time and/or as homework assignments. Provide them with the Writing Checklists on pages 112–113 to help them evaluate, revise, and edit their work.

Grade 1 Observational Writing Assessment Checklist

Student _____   Grade _____

Teacher _____   Date _____

Directions: Use this checklist to document students' writing progress throughout the year and to identify behaviors, skills, and strategies to support or validate during independent writing and conferring time.

Behaviors, Strategies, and Skills to Observe and Support	Date:	Date:	Date:	Date:	Date:
Stages of Writing Development					
Scribble Stage					
Isolated Letter Stage					
Transitional Stage					
Stylized Sentence Stage					
Writing Stage					
Fluent Stage					
Stages of Spelling Development					
Pre-Phonetic: Scribble writing					
Pre-Phonetic: Symbols					
Pre-Phonetic: Random letters					
Semi-Phonetic: Initial consonants					
Semi-Phonetic: Initial/final consonants					
Semi-Phonetic: Vowel/consonant combination in CVC words with inconsistently correct vowels (put, pot)					
Semi-Phonetic: Vowel/consonant combination in CVC words with correct use of vowels					
Transitional					
Correct Stage					
Concepts About Print/Print Conventions					
Print carries meaning					
Beginning of text					
One-to-one correspondence					
Spaces between words					
Directionality					
Uppercase letter at beginning of sentence					
Punctuation at the end of sentence					
Rereads from beginning of sentence					
Book titles underlined					
Composing/Writing Fluency					
Generates topics with teacher or peer support					
Holds the message in memory while writing					
Rereads to remember the next word in the message					
Writes a simple message of one to three sentences					
Avoids overused words					
Demonstrates writer's voice					
Varies sentence beginnings					
Spells several one-syllable and high-frequency words correctly					

(continued)

Grade 1 Observational Writing Assessment Checklist
(continued)

Behaviors, Strategies, and Skills to Observe and Support	Date:	Date:	Date:	Date:	Date:
Transcribing/Encoding					
Says words slowly to listen for sounds					
Hears and records sounds in words					
Attends to letter formation					
Language and Grammar					
Uses complete sentences in oral conversation					
Writes a complete sentence					
Capitalizes *I* and people's names within a sentence					
Uses accurate adjectives					
Orally composes complete sentences with compound subjects that include the pronoun *I*					
Writes complete sentences with compound subjects that include the pronoun *I*					
Uses personal pronouns after naming a person, group, or object					
Opinion/Argument Writing					
States an opinion or position					
Supports opinion or argument with evidence from the text					
Describes the setting					
Organizes idea in an appropriate sequence					
Provides some sense of closure					
Informative/Explanatory Writing					
Identifies the topic					
Writes topic sentence that states main idea					
Includes two or more facts from text					
Provides some sense of closure					
Narrative Writing					
Includes main character					
Includes other characters					
Includes a beginning, middle, and end					
Includes a problem in the narrative					
Develops a resolution to the problem					

NOTES:

The Developmental Stages of Writing

Scribble Stage: A student operating in the scribble stage writes with lines, scribbles, or mock-letter forms. He or she has no specific concept of the use of space on the page.

Isolated Letter Stage: During the isolated letter stage, letter forms begin to appear. Random letters and numbers recur throughout the writing sample, based on the student's developing knowledge. The student is still confused about such early concepts as words, directionality, and the use of space.

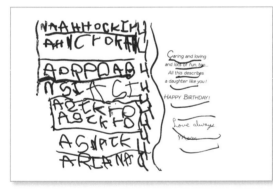

Transitional Stage: Some letter–sound correspondences and correctly spelled words begin to appear as the student moves into the transitional stage. However, they may be mixed with isolated letters and numerals.

Stylized Sentence Stage: As a student acquires a core writing vocabulary of frequently used words, he or she begins to use these words to construct sentences with simple patterns. The student is also beginning to refine concepts of spacing and letter–sound correspondence.

Writing Stage: A student moves beyond the stylized sentence stage as he or she learns to compose stories and acquires a larger writing vocabulary. The student uses more conventional spelling, longer sentences, and punctuation.

Fluent Stage: Fluent writers begin to develop strategies for the craft of writing. These strategies include elaborating (voice), critiquing their own writing and others' writing, writing in different genres, using what they know about reading text to write, using the writing process, and developing a sense of audience. Fluent writers spell most words correctly and carefully edit their spelling while they write. They also have a wide vocabulary and know how to use a thesaurus and dictionary to expand their current vocabulary. Fluent writers understand text structures. They write on a wide variety of topics, including personal experiences and nonfiction topics.

118

Evaluation Rubrics

Student _____   Grade _____

Teacher _____   Date _____

Opinion/Argument				
Traits	1	2	3	4
The writer states a strong opinion.				
The writer supplies reasons that support his or her opinion.				
The writer provides a sense of closure.				
The writer demonstrates command of grade-appropriate conventions of standard English.				

Informative/Explanatory				
Traits	1	2	3	4
The writer introduces his or her topic with a main idea statement.				
The writer uses facts and details to develop the topic.				
The writer provides a sense of closure.				
The writer demonstrates command of grade-appropriate conventions of standard English.				

Narrative				
Traits	1	2	3	4
The writer recounts two or more events.				
The writer includes details about what happened.				
The writer uses temporal words to signal event order.				
The writer provides a sense of closure to the narrative.				
The writer demonstrates command of grade-appropriate conventions of standard English.				

Key
1–Beginning
2–Developing
3–Accomplished
4–Exemplary

Comments

Opinion/Argument

TRAITS	1: Goal Oriented
The writer states a strong opinion.	When I start an opinion/argument piece, I state my opinion. I need to tell exactly what I think. After reading this prompt, I can state my opinion as ____.
The writer supplies reasons that support his or her opinion.	I need to think of good reasons to support my opinion. My opinion about this prompt is ____. I need to support my opinion with reasons I find in the text. Then I'll go back to my writing and include them.
The writer provides a sense of closure.	When I finish writing an opinion, I need to finish with a strong statement. I will say my opinion again.
The writer demonstrates command of grade-appropriate conventions of standard English.	I am going to read through my writing to make sure that I formed and used both regular and irregular verbs correctly. I will read through my whole opinion/argument piece to make sure that I have spelled words correctly.

2: Directive and Corrective Feedback	3: Self-Monitoring and Reflection	4: Validating and Confirming
Did you clearly state an opinion that answers the prompt? Revise your statement to make it clear and focused.	Tell me how you chose ____ as your opinion.	I can see that your opinion is ____. You made your opinion very clear.
What are your reasons for your opinion? Find details in the text for each reason.	How did you decide to organize your ideas? Did you identify the information that was most important to include? How did you do this?	You included some strong reasons to support your opinion.
Reread the last part of your opinion piece. Does it end by restating your point of view? Go back and look at your opinion statement. How can you say this again in another way?	How does your ending support your opinion? Is there a way you could make this conclusion stronger?	Your opinion had a great ending. You've really convinced me that your point of view makes sense.
Read that sentence again. Does it sound right to you? How should you change that? When you write a title, what do you need to do?	Show me a place in your writing where you used punctuation correctly. What rule did you follow?	Your opinion/argument piece included complete sentences, and you remembered all the end punctuation. I noticed you spelled many difficult words correctly.

Informative/Explanatory

TRAITS	1: Goal Oriented
The writer introduces his or her topic with a main idea statement.	When I start an informative/explanatory text, I introduce my topic. I'm going to think about what I want my readers to know about ____. Then I create a main idea statement.
The writer uses facts and details to develop the topic.	I need to find facts and details from the text to support my points. I can go back to the text and underline parts that I think will help my writing. Then I will include them in my informative/explanatory text.
The writer provides a sense of closure.	When I finish writing an informative/explanatory text, I need to summarize my ideas in a conclusion. I can look back at my main idea statement, then restate it as ____.
The writer demonstrates command of grade-appropriate conventions of standard English.	I am going to read through my writing to make sure that I used capital letters at the beginning of sentences.

2: Directive and Corrective Feedback	3: Self-Monitoring and Reflection	4: Validating and Confirming
How could you introduce your topic in a way that tells exactly what you will be writing about?	Take a look at your main idea statement. Do you feel that it clearly introduces your topic?	Your main idea statement is clearly ____. That introduction helped me understand exactly what I was going to read about.
What are your main points? Find supporting details and evidence in the text for each point.	Have you included all of the facts you wanted to share about ____?	You included some strong facts, definitions, and details to support your topic.
Reread the last sentences of your informative/explanatory text. Do they restate your main idea?	Show me your concluding statement. Is there a way you could make this conclusion stronger?	After I read your conclusion, I felt I had really learned something from your writing.
Read that sentence again. Does it sound right to you? Your verb is not [singular/plural]. How should you edit it?	Show me places in your writing where you used different kinds of end punctuation.	Your informative/explanatory text included the names of people and/or places and you remembered to capitalize them.

Narrative

TRAITS	1: Goal Oriented
The writer recounts two or more events.	I will use a chart to jot down the order of events I will write about. I will record details from the text I have already read. I will include those details in my new narrative.
The writer includes details about what happened.	I want to include descriptions in my narrative. I will write down words that will help my readers picture what I am writing about. Then I will include these in my narrative.
The writer uses temporal words to signal event order.	When I write a narrative, I need to use time words so that my reader does not get confused. I will add words and phrases such as *first, then, next,* and *last* to help my reader understand the order of events.
The writer provides a sense of closure to the narrative.	I am going to reread the ending of my narrative to make sure that it gives the reader a feeling that it is over. I need to concentrate on how the problem in the narrative is solved.
The writer demonstrates command of grade-appropriate conventions of standard English.	I am going to read through my narrative to make sure that I formed and used verbs correctly. I am going to scan through my narrative to make sure I used end punctuation on every sentence.

2: Directive and Corrective Feedback	3: Self-Monitoring and Reflection	4: Validating and Confirming
Think of events that will lead from the problem to the resolution. You've decided to write about ____. Now think of the sequence of events you will include.	What graphic organizer could help you organize your narrative events? Tell me how you went about organizing your narrative.	The events you organized lead to a [fun, surprising, etc.] resolution.
Imagine that you're a character. What's happening in the narrative? What do you have to say to other characters? What do you have to say about the events?	Show me how you gave information about your characters and setting.	I can visualize where your narrative takes place. You've included some nice descriptive details.
Let's read this paragraph. Is it clear to the reader when all the action is taking place? What words could you add to help the reader's understanding?	Show me where you used time words in your narrative. Show me a place where you could use time words to make the order of events clearer.	The phrase ____ gave me a good understanding of the order.
Let's read the ending of your narrative. Does it show how the problem is solved? Is there something you can add to make sure the reader feels as if the narrative piece is over?	Show me how your ending helps the reader know it is over.	You've developed an interesting resolution to the problem in your narrative.
I got confused about the sequence when ____. Take another look at your verb tenses. Make sure they are in the past tense when they should be. When you write a title, what do you need to do?	Show me a place in your writing where your sentences could be better. What could you do to improve them? Show me a sentence in which you changed the punctuation. How did you know it was wrong?	Your narrative included a lot of dialogue, and you used quotation marks correctly. I notice you spelled many difficult words correctly!

Editing/Proofreading Symbols

Mark	What It Means	How to Use It
ℓ	Delete. Take something out here.	We went to to the store.
∧	Change or insert letter or word.	San Francico, Calafornia my home.
#	Add a space here.	My familyloves to watch baseball.
⌒	Remove space.	We saw the sail boat streak by.
ℓ	Delete and close the space.	I gave the man my monney.
¶	Begin a new paragraph here.	"How are you?" I asked. "Great," said Jack.
⌐⌐	No new paragraph. Keep sentences together.	The other team arrived at one. The game started at once.
∼	Transpose (switch) the letters or words.	Thier friends came with gifts.
≡	Make this a capital letter.	mrs. smith
/	Make this a lowercase letter.	My Sister went to the City.
◯	Spell it out.	Mr. García has 3 cats.
⊙	Insert a period.	We ran home There was no time to spare
∧	Insert a comma.	We flew to Washington D.C.
∨	Insert an apostrophe.	Matts hat looks just like Johns.
∨∨	Insert quotation marks.	Hurry! said Brett.
?	Is this correct? Check it.	The Civil War ended in 1875. ?
STET	Ignore the edits. Leave as is.	Her hair was brown. STET

Common Core Writing to Texts Grade 1 • ©2014 Newmark Learning, LLC

Notes:

Notes:

Common Core Writing to Texts Grade 1 • ©2014 Newmark Learning, LLC